Major
Unsolved Crimes

CRIME, JUSTICE, AND PUNISHMENT

Major
Unsolved Crimes

Phelan Powell

Austin Sarat, GENERAL EDITOR

CHELSEA HOUSE PUBLISHERS
Philadelphia

Frontis: *Scotland Yard displays lost Jack the Ripper documents.*

Chelsea House Publishers

Editor in Chief Stephen Reginald
Managing Editor James D. Gallagher
Production Manager Pamela Loos
Art Director Sara Davis
Director of Photography Judy L. Hasday
Senior Production Editor LeeAnne Gelletly

Staff for MAJOR UNSOLVED CRIMES

Associate Art Director Takeshi Takahashi
Picture Researcher Patricia Burns
Cover Illustrator Janet Hamlin

3 5 7 9 8 6 4 2

The Chelsea House World Wide Web site address is
http://www.chelseahouse.com

Library of Congress Cataloging-in-Publication Data

Powell, Phelan.
Major unsolved crimes / Phelan Powell; Austin Sarat, general
editor
    p.   cm. — (Crime, justice, and punishment)
Includes bibliographical references.
Summary: Discusses six criminal cases in which there was no
completely satisfactory conclusion reached, including the case
of the Zodiac killer, the Tylenol murderer, the assassination of
President Kennedy, and an unusual skyjacking in 1971.

ISBN 0-7910-4277-4 (hc)

1. Crime case studies Juvenile literature. 2. Serial murderers
Case studies Juvenile literature. [1. Murder Case studies. 2.
Crime Case studies.] I. Sarat, Austin. II. Title III. Series
HV6251.P68   1999
364.15'23—dc21   99-24140
                                                      CIP

Contents

CRIME, JUSTICE, AND PUNISHMENT

Fears and Fascinations:

An Introduction to
Crime, Justice, and Punishment

By Austin Sarat

We live with crime and images of crime all around us. Crime evokes in most of us a deep aversion, a feeling of profound vulnerability, but it also evokes an equally deep fascination. Today, in major American cities the fear of crime is a major fact of life, some would say a disproportionate response to the realities of crime. Yet the fear of crime is real, palpable in the quickened steps and furtive glances of people walking down darkened streets. At the same time, we eagerly follow crime stories on television and in movies. We watch with a "who done it" curiosity, eager to see the illicit deed done, the investigation undertaken, the miscreant brought to justice and given his just deserts. On the streets the presence of crime is a reminder of our own vulnerability and the precariousness of our taken-for-granted rights and freedoms. On television and in the movies the crime story gives us a chance to probe our own darker motives, to ask "Is there a criminal within?" as well as to feel the collective satisfaction of seeing justice done.

Fear and fascination, these two poles of our engagement with crime, are, of course, only part of the story. Crime is, after all, a major social and legal problem, not just an issue of our individual psychology. Politicians today use our fear of, and fascination with, crime for political advantage. How we respond to crime, as well as to the political uses of the crime issue, tells us a lot about who we are as a people as well as what we value and what we tolerate. Is our response compassionate or severe? Do we seek to understand or to punish, to enact an angry vengeance or to rehabilitate and welcome the criminal back into our midst? The CRIME, JUSTICE, AND PUNISHMENT series is designed to explore these themes, to ask why we are fearful and fascinated, to probe the meanings and motivations of crimes and criminals and of our responses to them, and, finally, to ask what we can learn about ourselves and the society in which we live by examining our responses to crime.

Crime is always a challenge to the prevailing normative order and a test of the values and commitments of law-abiding people. It is sometimes a Raskolnikov-like act of defiance, an assertion of the unwillingness of some to live according to the rules of conduct laid out by organized society. In this sense, crime marks the limits of the law and reminds us of law's all-too-regular failures. Yet sometimes there is more desperation than defiance in criminal acts; sometimes they signal a deep pathology or need in the criminal. To confront crime is thus also to come face-to-face with the reality of social difference, of class privilege and extreme deprivation, of race and racism, of children neglected, abandoned, or abused whose response is to enact on others what they have experienced themselves. And occasionally crime, or what is labeled a criminal act, represents a call for justice, an appeal to a higher moral order against the inadequacies of existing law.

Figuring out the meaning of crime and the motivations of criminals and whether crime arises from defiance, desperation, or the appeal for justice is never an easy task. The motivations and meanings of crime are as varied as are the persons who engage in criminal conduct. They are as mysterious as any of the mysteries of the human soul. Yet the desire to know the secrets of crime and the criminal is a strong one, for in that knowledge may lie one step on the road to protection, if not an assurance of one's own personal safety. Nonetheless, as strong as that desire may be, there is no available technology that can allow us to know the whys of crime with much confidence, let alone a scientific certainty. We can, however, capture something about crime by studying the defiance, desperation, and quest for justice that may be associated with it. Books in the CRIME, JUSTICE, AND PUNISHMENT series will take up that challenge. They tell stories of crime and criminals, some famous, most not, some glamorous and exciting, most mundane and commonplace.

This series will, in addition, take a sober look at American criminal justice, at the procedures through which we investigate crimes and identify criminals, at the institutions in which innocence or guilt is determined. In these procedures and institutions we confront the thrill of the chase as well as the challenge of protecting the rights of those who defy our laws. It is through the efficiency and dedication of law enforcement that we might capture the criminal; it is in the rare instances of their corruption or brutality that we feel perhaps our deepest betrayal. Police, prosecutors, defense lawyers, judges, and jurors administer criminal justice and in their daily actions give substance to the guarantees of the Bill of Rights. What is an adversarial system of justice? How does it work? Why do we have it? Books in the CRIME, JUSTICE, AND PUNISHMENT series will examine the thrill of the chase as we seek to capture the criminal. They will also reveal the drama and majesty of the criminal trial as well as the day-to-day reality of a criminal justice system in which trials are the exception and negotiated pleas of guilty are the rule.

When the trial is over or the plea has been entered, when we have separated the innocent from the guilty, the moment of punishment has arrived. The injunction to punish the guilty, to respond to pain inflicted by inflicting pain, is as old as civilization itself. "An eye for an eye and a tooth for a tooth" is a biblical reminder that punishment must measure pain for pain. But our response to the criminal must be better than and different from the crime itself. The biblical admonition, along with the constitutional prohibition of "cruel and unusual punishment," signals that we seek to punish justly and to be just not only in the determination of who can and should be punished, but in how we punish as well. But neither reminder tells us what to do with the wrongdoer. Do we rape the rapist, or burn the home of the arsonist? Surely justice and decency say no. But, if not, then how can and should we punish? In a world in which punishment is neither identical to the crime nor an automatic response to it, choices must be made and we must make them. Books in the CRIME, JUSTICE, AND PUNISHMENT series will examine those choices and the practices, and politics, of punishment. How do we punish and why do we punish as we do? What can we learn about the rationality and appropriateness of today's responses to crime by examining our past and its responses? What works? Is there, and can there be, a just measure of pain?

CRIME, JUSTICE, AND PUNISHMENT brings together books on some of the great themes of human social life. The books in this series capture our fear and fascination with crime and examine our responses to it. They remind us of the deadly seriousness of these subjects. They bring together themes in law, literature, and popular culture to challenge us to think again, to think anew, about subjects that go to the heart of who we are and how we can and will live together.

*   *   *   *   *

Where there is crime ideally there should be justice. The perpetrator should be identified, apprehended, judged, and punished. But this ideal is by no means always attained. Many crimes, some serious, some less so, remain unsolved, frustrating those who were victimized and those whose job it is to enforce the law. Generally, however, scholars have ignored these unsolved crimes, focusing instead on the processing of crimes for which arrests are made. *Major Unsolved Crimes* repairs this omission. It tells the gripping stories of a series of unsolved crimes, from Jack the Ripper to the sabotage of the Sunset Limited, highlighting the personalities involved and the contexts in which those crimes occurred.

This book will provide good reading for those fascinated by crime. It raises a variety of intriguing questions such as: What counts as an unsolved crime? Is an unsolved crime one for which there has been no official "clearance" of the crime? Or, is there something else that is at work? Are there certain kinds of crimes that are more difficult to resolve than others? How typical is the "unsolved crime"? Do crimes remain unsolved because of the ingenuity of their perpetrators or the incompetence of police?

The crimes on which this book focused are some of the most celebrated in British and American history. They compel our attention both because of the daring shown and because the crime remains unsolved. All of us can learn a lot about crime, law enforcement, and the culture in which we live by attending to these unsolved crimes.

Detective Dave Toschi of the San Francisco Police Department
searches through files on the Zodiac killer. Despite a massive law
enforcement effort, the serial murderer was never caught.

Six major crimes. Five unsolved and one laid to an uneasy rest. Unsolved crimes are the nemesis of every law enforcement official whose task is to bring the perpetrators to justice. The cases capture the imagination of amateur sleuths, who collect the clues available to them through the press and attempt to solve the crimes on their own. Violent unsolved murders such as the three following cases terrorize us by their fierce and random nature, preying on our fear that any one of us might be a criminal's next victim.

It was in the early morning of August 31, 1888, that Mary Ann Nichols, known to friends and acquaintances as "Polly," wandered drunk and penniless down Whitechapel Road in London's East End. She was accustomed to procuring money for her night's lodging by engaging strangers in brief sexual trysts. About 2:30 A.M., Ellen Holland, a friend and former roommate of Polly's, saw the inebriated woman and tried to persuade her to come home with her. Polly declined, confident that she would find a customer in a short time and have money enough to find her own place to stay for what was left of the night. Within the hour, Polly was dead. Her throat had been cut and she had been brutally disemboweled. Polly had become the first of many victims of Jack the Ripper, a killer whose name would echo down the decades and fascinate criminologists a hundred years after his deeds were committed. To this day, the crimes of Jack the Ripper remain unsolved.

Almost 80 years later, high school students Betty Lou Jensen and David Faraday drove to a lovers lane in a remote area of northern California. A gunman approached Faraday's car and, as the teenagers attempted to flee, shot both dead. They were two of what would become six victims of "Zodiac," a killer in the San Francisco area during the late 1960s. Zodiac would eventually claim to have killed as many as 37 victims, most of whom were young women. Over the years, the police have investigated more than 2,500 suspects, and although one or two surfaced as likely to be the Zodiac killer, no one has ever been arrested for the Zodiac murders.

Death struck Chicago's West Side in 1982 when a murderer poisoned a popular pain reliever. The Tylenol killer did not even know who his victims were until their deaths were reported in the media. He did not know until after the fact that one person who swallowed a cyanide-laden capsule, taken from a bottle of Tylenol, would be a child. Seven victims fell prey to the poison inserted into Tylenol products and returned to store shelves for consumer purchase.

In the past, police found most murders could be solved because they had been motivated by common emotions such as jealousy, greed, revenge, profit, or anger. The murderous rampage would cease after the murderer had released his emotional baggage. In cases such as these, the murderer made little attempt to cover his or her tracks. In fact, today police statistics show that 80 percent of homicides are still committed by someone the victim knew. Usually spontaneous, unplanned acts, the murders tend to be committed by people who are full of remorse once they realize what they have done. But in many cases, people are being killed by strangers, who leave little or no evidence of motive at the scene of the crime.

Jack the Ripper, Zodiac, and the Tylenol killer showed careful planning in their murders. A killer's *modus operandi* is the manner or weapon used to commit the crime. A killer's signature is what the killer *needs* to do to make the murder a fulfilling experience for himself. The Zodiac killer could change his modus operandi of inflicting death either by gunshot or knife. But he always needed to come face-to-face with the terror in the eyes of his victims to enjoy his emotional fulfillment from the murders. Jack the Ripper and the Zodiac needed to kill their victims at close range. Yet the killer who planted poisoned drugs on store shelves did not need to watch his or her victims suffer in order to gratify the killer instincts.

The art of police profiling of criminals, particularly of serial murderers, has advanced over the years. Police profilers attempt to put themselves into the minds of the criminals to understand what motivates them. Profilers agree that a major motivation of all serial killers is the need to achieve power and control over their victims. Serial killers tend to blend into society because they are often very likeable, but they tend to be incapable of normal, healthy relationships, particularly with the opposite sex. They often have a history of animal abuse and teenage bed-wetting.

Initially, mutilation of animals provides adequate fulfillment, but eventually it is not enough and the killers graduate to human victims to satisfy their sexual fantasies. These murderers feel no guilt for their crimes, and they will place the blame on others. Their crimes seldom stop until they are caught or dead. The randomness of such crimes is our terror, and the randomness of such crimes is the killer's gratification and pleasure.

Of course, crimes with random victims aren't limited to serial murder. Terrorist plots have been carried out recently in the United States, as yet another threat to our peace of mind and safety. Some attacks, such as the April 1995 Oklahoma City bombing, have even been the work of disgruntled U.S. citizens. Unlike the Oklahoma City bombing, which was solved fairly quickly, however, the sabotage of Amtrak's Sunset Limited train in October 1995 has not been solved. The masterminds of this crime, which sent the train plunging down a ravine in Arizona, probably expected a death and injury toll greater than the one person killed and 78 injured. Law enforcement officials are still searching for the terrorists responsible.

A unique unsolved crime included in this book is the D. B. Cooper airliner hijacking. It differs from the other crimes in that no one was hurt, except perhaps Cooper; no one had ever committed such an audacious crime before; and no one has since. In 1971, D. B. Cooper became something of a folk hero rather than a criminal to be feared. He hijacked an airliner and parachuted out with $200,000. It was not hard for the average citizen to appreciate his desire for a pile of cash with no strings attached. Police diligence turned up almost 10,000 suspects and created a 60-volume case file. But the true identity of the skyjacker, who jumped from an airliner two miles above British Columbia, Canada, has never been discovered.

Was Cooper the hijacker's real name? Had he selected the skyjacked airliner at random? Did he survive his parachute jump from the tail of a three-engine, passenger jetliner? We may never know.

The last of our unsolved cases is the Kennedy assassination. This is a murder case that is under constant discussion, thought by some to be solved but by many not to be. Lee Harvey Oswald was arrested shortly after the assassination of the 35th president of the United States on November 22, 1963. Two days later, Lee Harvey Oswald was dead, shot point-blank as he was being escorted from a Dallas, Texas, police station. One year later, the Warren Commission released an 888-page report that concluded Oswald alone had murdered

John F. Kennedy. Many eyewitness accounts from people who were near the president's motorcade before, during, and after the assassination indicate that if Oswald did shoot at the president, he was not the only one who did so that day. These accounts, and evidence contradicting the Warren Commission's findings, have helped to relegate this crime to the category of unsolved.

So, with the possible exception of the assassination of President Kennedy, all of these cases have remained open, one for more than a century. But perhaps one day in the 21st century, someone will whisper a deathbed confession that he or she has an alias of Zodiac, or put cyanide in Chicago's Tylenol, or even fired that fourth shot that rang out through Dallas so long ago. Until then these cases remain part of the world's major unsolved crimes.

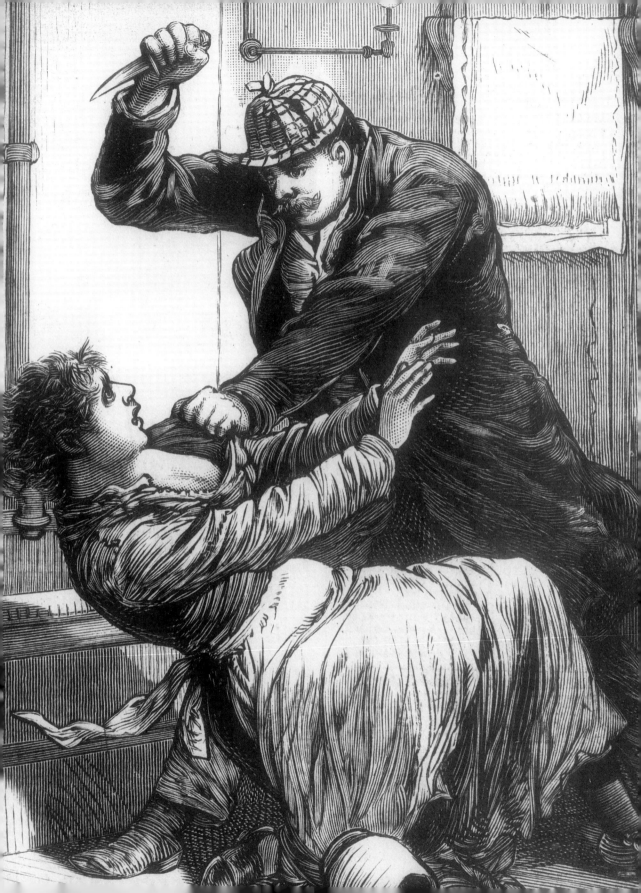

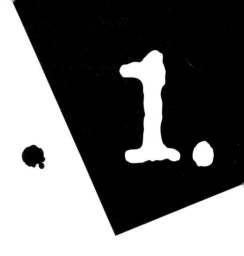

JACK THE RIPPER

Police in 19th century London considered a 43-year-old prostitute named Mary Ann "Polly" Nichols to be Jack the Ripper's first victim.

Charles Cross was on his way to his job as a carman in the early hours of August 31, 1888, when he made a gruesome discovery in the alley of a place called Buck's Row in the East End of London. What he first thought was a heap of cloth lying on the side of the road turned out to be the body of a woman.

At 3:40 A.M., Cross was joined by fellow carman Robert Paul, who was also on his way to work. Cross thought the woman might still be alive. The two men left the scene to seek a policeman. They told the first officer they saw that the woman was probably drunk. But when the officer arrived he realized that the woman's throat had been cut and that she was dead. He summoned more police and an ambulance.

A doctor arrived and officially declared the woman

Mary Ann "Polly" Nichols was the first victim of the English serial killer Jack the Ripper. Mary Ann had been a London prostitute as were his other four victims.

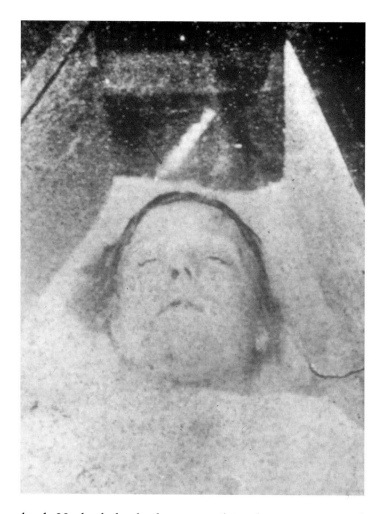

dead. He had the body removed to the mortuary and went back home. An hour later, when Inspector John Spratling arrived at the murder site, the body was gone and someone had washed the sidewalk area clear of blood and any other evidence that might have aided police efforts.

Polly's murderer had knifed her so severely in the neck that her vertebrae were exposed. She was stabbed numerous times and also disemboweled. Police interrogated hundreds of people who lived or worked in the London area where Polly Nichols died but the investi-

The murders by Jack the Ripper became the lead story of the day, breeding fear, greed, and community outrage.

gators came up blank. No one had seen or heard anything at the time of the murder.

Two days after Nichols was buried, the body of Annie Chapman, a 47-year-old prostitute, was found in the East End of London. Her real name was Eliza Anne Smith. In the early morning of September 8, 1888, Annie had been seen alive near Hanbury Street. However, within the hour, John Davis found Annie Chapman lying along the fence at the rear of his premises, dead. The scene was a gruesome one. Her dress was above her knees; her intestines were draped across her left shoulder. Her abdomen had been sliced open and organs were missing from her corpse.

Inspector Frederick George Abberline connected this latest killing with the Nichols case. Scotland Yard soon flooded the area with uniformed police and plain-clothesmen. Some of the policemen were even disguised as women to lure the killer to them.

After Chapman's death, more police had to be assigned to crowd control in the East End than were working on the actual investigation. Residents realized that money could be made from the curious who came by the hundreds to view the murder sites. The tickets sold granted the purchaser a full view of the spot where Chapman died. Food was sold to hungry onlookers.

Several citizens groups were formed to help the police. One was called the Mile End Vigilance Committee. The committee posted notices throughout the district asking anyone with information about the killings to come forward. The committee offered a reward for any tips leading to the arrest and conviction of the murderer.

In the early morning hours of September 30, Louis Diemschutz was traveling down London's Berner Street on his donkey-pulled cart when the wheels of the cart rolled over something. When Diemschutz jumped down to see what it was, he saw the body of a woman. Blood was still running from her neck where her head was almost cut off. Diemschutz ran to a near-by club to get help. In a short time, the area was full of spectators. The body was identified as Elizabeth Stride, a prostitute.

At about the same time, P. C. Watkins of the London police was patroling the southern part of the East End. Watkins knew nothing of the body that had just been found by Diemschutz. As he walked his beat through Mitre Square, Watkins was suddenly brought up short by the sight of a body lying in his path. He saw a woman whose throat had been cut.

The method of the murderer was gruesome and Scotland Yard had its hands full trying to solve the case before someone else died. Here the body of the third victim, Elizabeth Stride, is found.

Her stomach had been savagely torn open, and her intestines had been pulled out and draped over her right shoulder. She was identified as prostitute Catherine Eddowes.

One of Catherine Eddowes kidneys had been ripped from her body and was missing from the crime scene. A short time later, a postcard was delivered to the police. It was from the murderer. He wrote about how Elizabeth Stride had "squealed" as he cut her and how he did not have a chance to get her ears. He bragged about the murders of Elizabeth and Catherine as a "double event."

Mitre Square as it appears today. It was here that the gruesome murder of Catherine Eddowes took place.

During Stride's inquest, an attempt at "profiling" the murderer appeared in a local paper. A doctor wrote in offering the theory that the killer might be suffering from the delusion that he had a godly duty to eradicate vice; therefore, he killed prostitutes.

Several days after the murders, George Lusk, the chairman of the Whitechapel Vigilance Committee, received a box in the mail. Lusk opened the box and to his horror discovered part of Catherine Eddowes's missing kidney. The enclosed note challenged, "Catch me if you can, Mr. Lusk." The killer bragged that he had eaten the rest of Eddowes's kidney. "It was very nice," was his gruesome critique. He promised to send Lusk the bloody knife that had cut the kidney from the prostitute's body "if you only wate a whil longer." [Original spelling.]

On September 27 the Central News Agency of London had received a letter written with red ink. The recipients considered the letter a joke and did nothing with it for a couple of days until someone decided it should probably be turned over to the police.

It read (including the original misspellings):

> Dear Boss,
> I keep on hearing, the police have caught me but they wont fix me just yet. I have laughed when they look so clever and talk about being on the right track. I am down on whores and I shant quit ripping them till I do get buckled. Grand work the last job was. I gave the lady no time to squeal. How can they catch me now. I love my work and want to start again. You will soon hear of me with my funny little games. I saved some of the proper red stuff in a ginger beer bottle over the last job to write with but it went thick like glue and I cant use it. Red ink is fit enough I hope ha ha. The next job I do I shall clip the ladys ears off and send to the police officers just for jolly wouldn't you. Keep this letter back till I do a bit more work then give it out straight. My knife's so nice and sharp I want to get to work right away if I get a chance. Good luck.
> Yours truly
> Jack the Ripper
> Don't mind giving me the trade name.

The day after the double murders of Stride and Eddowes, the Central News Agency received a postcard that was delivered immediately to the police. It was apparent that the writer was the same one who wrote the earlier letter. This message was also written in red ink:

> I was not codding dear old Boss when I gave you the tip, youll hear about saucy Jacky's work tomorrow double event this time number one squealed a bit couldn't finish straight off had not time to get ears for police thanks for keeping last letter back till I got to work again.
> Jack the Ripper

Montague John Druitt was one of the many suspects in the Ripper investigation, drawing suspicion because the murders stopped after he drowned.

At long last, the killer had a name, but not a face.

The four killings had occurred within a month's span, ending with Eddowes's death September 30. The public had just begun to relax from the terror of the Ripper when on November 9, 1888, the most brutal of all the murders occurred.

Known by the nicknames "Black Mary," "Fair Emma," and "Ginger," Mary Jeanette Kelly was a London prostitute like the other victims. Kelly's murder was the only killing by the Ripper that took place off the streets of London. She was found viciously mutilated in her room. Parts of her body had been removed and placed at various points around her body. Police surgeon Dr. Thomas Bond believed that the mutilation of Kelly must have taken several hours. Her heart was never found. When she died, Kelly was pregnant.

Speculation centered on the surgical nature of the killings. It was thought that the assailant might have been someone with medical training. Rumor had it that a mad doctor was the killer.

Another theory was that Jack might actually be a "Jill," a mad midwife who was killing the prostitutes to practice her abortion techniques. Scotland Yard rejected this notion because criminologists said that no woman had ever been linked to mutilation murders.

The list of suspects included a man named Montague John Druitt. He was a down-and-out lawyer, fished out of the Thames River in December 1888, a short time after Jack the Ripper's last murder.

Two other men suspected of the killings were already murderers. Severin Klosowski and Dr. Thomas Neil Cream had killed women with poison. Klosowski also went under the name George Chapman. He had poisoned three of his wives. Eventually imprisoned for the third murder, which occurred in 1902, Chapman was executed for that crime. Police believed that he was probably their best Ripper suspect because he had been trained as a surgeon.

The other suspect, Dr. Cream, who was known to be a murderer, was in an American jail at the time of the murders. However, as he was being hanged for his poisoning crimes, he was heard to mumble, "I am Jack . . . ."

The search for Jack the Ripper even led investigators to His Royal Highness Prince Albert Victor, Duke of Clarence, grandson of Queen Victoria. The police had no hard evidence against the prince. But in their frantic search for the killer, the police were pursuing all leads with equal vigor.

Police also suspected three men close to the prince of having been involved in the murders. Sir William Gult was the royal physician. He and a royal artist, Walter Sickert, and a royal coachman were believed to have committed the murders to cover up an indiscretion by the prince with one of the prostitutes. The prince himself was cleared of the crimes when police realized that he had been nowhere near the sites of the killings when they occurred.

Yet another suspect was Dr. Francis Tumblety, who was not a licensed doctor at all. He was so seriously considered a possible Ripper that Scotland Yard Inspector Walter Andrews traveled to America in 1889 to question him in New York. Born in Ireland, Tumblety had moved to New York when he was a child. He had traveled extensively throughout the United States and had visited England, Ireland, and Scotland. In the early

The police files on the Jack the Ripper case, here being held by a member of Scotland Yard in 1987, have been studied extensively for clues to the identity of this notorious murderer.

1880s, Tumblety had a male acquaintance whom he warned against women, particularly prostitutes.

Tumblety had been in London when the Ripper murders occurred and was connected to the Ripper slayings for two reasons. He had taken up lodging in houses near several of the slayings and acquaintances knew him to have a true hatred for women. Scotland Yard considered Tumblety a key suspect, although his description varied from witness accounts of men seen near the victims before they died. Tumblety stood 5 feet 10 inches tall and had a long, handlebar mustache. Most witnesses recalled seeing shorter men near the crime scenes. As with the other suspects, Scotland Yard never had enough evidence to arrest Tumblety.

In the late 1800s police policy at Scotland Yard was to discourage its officers from writing memoirs. This explains why little is known today about why certain suspects were deemed most likely to be the man who called himself Jack the Ripper.

Inspector Frederick George Abberline, who had joined the police department in 1863, was considered the most important member of the team who investigated the Ripper murders. Abberline firmly believed that Severin Klosowski (also known as George Chapman) was the murderer. When Klosowski was arrested, Abberline supposedly said to his fellow police officers, "You've got the Ripper at last." But Abberline later denied ever saying that.

Chief Inspector Henry Moore was in charge of the investigation of the Ripper murders and never stated in writing who he thought was a primary suspect.

Chief Inspector Walter Dew, the third member of the Ripper detective team, was one of the first detectives to break the memoir ban. Unfortunately, his writings revealed little new information, and he often failed to remember incidents as they were actually recorded in police reports.

More than 100 years after the gruesome murders, speculation over the identity of Jack the Ripper continues.

WANTED

SAN FRANCISCO POLICE DEPARTMENT

NO. 90-69   <u>WANTED FOR MURDER</u>   OCTOBER 18, 1969

ORIGINAL DRAWING   AMENDED DRAWING

Supplementing our Bulletin 87-69 of October 13, 1969. Additional information has developed the above amended drawing of murder suspect known as "ZODIAC".

WMA, 35-45 Years, approximately 5'8", Heavy Build, Short Brown Hair, possibly with Red Tint, Wears Glasses. Armed with 9 MM Automatic.

Available for comparison: Slugs, Casings, Latents, Handwriting.

<u>ANY INFORMATION:</u>
Inspectors Armstrong & Toschi
Homicide Detail
CASE NO. 696314

THOMAS J. CAHILL
CHIEF OF POLICE

The Zodiac Murders

The San Francisco Bay area of California became a place of terror in late 1968 and 1969. A killer stalked the area, calling himself the Zodiac killer. Six of his victims have been positively identified, although in letters he claims to have killed as many as 37 people over a period of five years.

The killer's first victims, 17-year-old David Faraday and his 16-year-old girlfriend, Betty Lou Jensen, lived near Vallejo, California. On the night of December 20, 1968, the two had told their parents that they were going to a school concert. But the teenagers actually went to a popular hangout for kids overlooking a lake.

They parked on the remote lovers lane even though police had often warned young people of the dangers in such an isolated spot. Within minutes of their arrival, another car pulled up next to them. The occupant of the car shot David in the head. When Betty Lou fled in terror from her assailant, he fired five shots into her body. Police could find no suspect in the

This wanted poster shows the composite sketch police eventually gleaned from descriptions by the few victims to survive the infamous Zodiac killer.

31

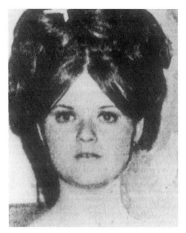  

The first known victims of Zodiac were from left to right: Betty Lou Jensen, David Faraday, and Darlene Ferrin. Darlene's boyfriend, Mike Mageau, survived the attack.

murders. The motive seemed to be killing for the sheer enjoyment of it.

Darlene Ferrin had known the two young victims. The day after their murders she told friends that although she had frequently visited the lovers lane where they were killed, she would never go there again.

Seven months later, on July 5, 1969, Darlene was sitting in a parking lot off a golf course with a friend, Mike Mageau. They were about two miles from the spot where David and Betty Lou had been killed. On the way to the parking lot, Darlene and Mike thought they were being followed, and they were right. A man approached their car and let loose with a barrage of bullets, which passed through Mike's arm and into Darlene's body. As Mike watched, the assailant started to walk away. The man then strode back to Mike's car and fired again.

Shortly after the attack, an unidentified man called the Vallejo police department. He said he wanted to report a double murder. (In fact, Darlene had died, but Mike lived.) After describing the location of the crime, the caller then also took credit for killing Faraday and Jensen the year before.

Soon afterwards, the *San Francisco Chronicle*

received a message from someone claiming to be the killer of Darlene, David, and Betty Lou. He gave details of the crime scenes that only the killer could have known. He signed the message with the symbol of a crossed circle and enclosed a paper on which was written one third of a coded message. The same letter with minor variations was sent to the *Vallejo Times–Herald* and the *San Francisco Examiner*. Both newspapers also received a different third of the ciphered message that had been sent to the *Chronicle*. The end of the letters sent to the latter two papers contained a threat. The killer said that if the cipher were not printed in the papers on August 1, 1969, he would go on a killing spree that night. He promised to kill as many as a dozen people by the end of the weekend. Portions of the letter were printed in the papers that day, but police elected to keep out details about the crimes that only the killer would know.

The 24 lines of the coded message were broken into 8 lines apiece. The code was composed of various symbols: Greek symbols, Morse code, weather symbols, alphabet characters, navy semaphore, and astrological symbols.

The police sent the cipher to U.S. Naval Intelligence to break the code. The agency had no luck. Throughout the San Francisco area, amateur code-breakers also tried to solve the cipher. Police work is sometimes aided by sheer luck and this time a husband and wife team took on the task and broke the code within 24 hours.

The deciphered message sent to the *Vallejo Times–Herald* read as follows:

> I like killing people because it is so much fun it is more fun than killing wild game in the forest because man is the most dangerous anamal of all to kill something gi. . .

The cipher sent to the *San Francisco Examiner* continued the message:

This cryptogram message was sent by the Zodiac killer to the San Francisco Chronicle. Like the letters of Jack the Ripper, Zodiac's communications taunted authorities and revealed a chillingly twisted mind.

ives me the most thrilling experience it is even better than getting your rocks off with a girl the best part of it is that when I die I will be reborn in paradice and all th. . .

And to the *San Francisco Chronicle*:

. . . e I have killed will become my slaves I will not give you my name because you will try to slow down or stop my collection of slaves for my after life e b e o r i e t e m e t h h p i t i.

The last line of the message was an undecipherable group of letters. The killer had informed the newspapers that if his code were broken, his identity would be revealed. But that did not happen.

Several days later, the killer wrote a three-page letter revealing more details of the killings. For the first time, he signed his letter with the name *Zodiac*.

The following September, Zodiac found his next victims. Cecilia Ann Shepard and Bryan Hartnell had been friends for years. She had been attending college in Napa County and was preparing to leave for southern California to continue her education. On a Saturday in September, the two decided to spend the day together. They drove to a lakeside and settled on a peninsula jutting into the lake. The beach area was deserted and no boats were sailing near the shore.

As the two lay in the sun and talked, Cecilia noticed a man in the distance behind some shrubbery. She mentioned the man to Bryan, and the two looked in that direction. Within a few minutes the man emerged from another direction; he was within a few feet of them. He had changed from an average-dressed man to a sinister figure clothed in a black hood. Slits were cut for his eyes and the hood came down in front of his chest. On his chest was stitched a circle overlaid with a cross.

The hooded figure stabbed the two young people repeatedly in front of each other. Cecilia was stabbed 24 times. Bryan lived. Cecilia did not.

A man claiming to be the Zodiac killer called into a TV station to talk with San Francisco attorney Melvin Belli (right) and talk-show host Jim Dunbar (left). Though they pleaded with him to surrender and he called several times, nothing came of it.

Psychiatrists studying the Zodiac killer's profile claimed he was probably a person cut off from society. They suggested that the killer was alienated to the point of thinking that people looked down on him. His belief that his victims would be his slaves in the afterlife indicated some paranoid delusion of grandeur.

The Zodiac killer wrote more than 20 letters to the press bragging about his deeds. Experts believed that his letters and phone calls, in which he claimed responsibility for his crimes, were actually attempts to be found out. They thought it was likely he would take his own life at some point. Although a plea was made to him in the press to turn himself in, the plea went unanswered.

Murders that could be definitively attributed to the Zodiac killer ended in 1969. But he would continue to taunt the public with his letters and mysterious ciphered messages until 1978. In the fall of 1969, the Zodiac killer wrote a letter to the *San Francisco Chron-*

icle. In it he claimed responsibility for the killing of a taxi driver and cited details of the crime only the police would know. He then threatened to kill schoolchildren in the Napa Valley of California by shooting out school bus tires and picking off the children, one by one, as they emerged from the buses.

News of this threat threw the public into a panic. Over the next months, police placed armed guards on school buses each day. It appeared that taunting the police and newspapers was a favorite sport of this demented killer.

Only one person is known to have come face-to-face with the Zodiac killer without being injured. Stopped on the road by car trouble, a woman with her infant child accepted an offer of help. Within moments of entering the stranger's car, the young mother realized that she was in the presence of a very dangerous man. As he sped down the road, the man described his plans to kill her. However, when the car slowed down on a freeway ramp, the woman had the presence of mind to escape.

With her child in her arms, the woman rushed into the streets of the nearby town and to the safety of the police station. As she told her terrifying story to the offi-

Three more Zodiac victims (left to right): San Francisco cab driver Paul Stine, Cecilia Shepard, and Bryan Hartnell. Hartnell survived multiple stab wounds; Stine and Shepard were not as fortunate.

The investigation into the killer's identity continues, with piles of material accumulated and detectives still unable to arrest anyone and close the case.

cer on duty, she looked at the wanted posters on the wall. The woman gasped when she recognized the composite sketch of the Zodiac killer. She realized that she had been in the presence of one of the most dangerous men in the country.

By 1983, the police had compiled files on 2,500 Zodiac suspects. All murders of young people in the geographical region of the original killings have been investigated thoroughly in order to establish or discard a Zodiac connection.

According to police, one man has remained the primary Zodiac suspect throughout the years. His identity has not been revealed, since police have never been able to link him to the crimes with physical evidence. But police were able to connect him to the time and place of the murders. His psychological makeup is a nightmare of deviant tendencies. In searches of his various living quarters, police have found writing samples that are similar to those sent to the press and signed "Zodiac." Aquaintances even claimed that, before the Zodiac killings began, this suspect had bragged to them that he would one day kill people and call himself the Zodiac. But police knew that such an admission, particularly secondhand, was not enough to legally warrant an arrest.

Speculation concerning the identity of Zodiac has ranged from pedestrian to preposterous. And the most probable suspect remains free. Where is Zodiac now? Are there recent unsolved murders for which he is responsible? Is he serving time in jail now for an unrelated crime, perhaps soon to be released to an unsuspecting world? Until someone is caught and convicted, or until he strikes again, we may never know.

CASH TO GO

The passengers on the airliner were relaxing moments after takeoff from Portland, Oregon, on the night before Thanksgiving 1971. A dark-clothed man, who called himself Dan Cooper, handed a note to the flight attendant. She did not look at the note, perhaps thinking it was a request for her phone number. The man leaned toward her and urged her to read it, saying he had a bomb. Inside his briefcase was a bundle of red sticks and wires.

Not many passengers were aboard this flight to Seattle, Washington, and none of them were aware that they were now part of a skyjacking. The plane landed as scheduled and the passengers left the plane at the Seattle-Tacoma International Airport, still unaware that the man in the dark suit had commandeered the plane and demanded that $200,000 and four parachutes

The adventure of D. B. Cooper was made into a movie by Polygram Pictures. Here actor Treat Williams reenacts his jump from a 727 at 10,000 feet.

be waiting for him at the Seattle airport. Cooper then wanted the pilot to fly the plane toward Mexico.

While the plane was on the ground in Seattle, FBI agents accumulated a bundle of $20 bills—10,000 in all. The lawmen photocopied the bills before handing the bundle over to the skyjacker. Although they did not know why Cooper wanted four parachutes, the agents feared he might take hostages and bail out of the plane with them.

After the empty plane was refueled, Cooper demanded four crew members to fly him to Mexico. He ordered the crew to fly no higher than 10,000 feet and no faster than 200 mph. Landing gear was to remain down and the wing flaps were to be set at 15 degrees. These measures would slow the airliner and make jumping from it easier. Once in the air, Cooper had the 126-passenger cabin to himself. He ordered the flight attendant to join the rest of the crew in the cockpit and stay there. As she was leaving, she saw Cooper strap the bags of money around his waist.

Before the plane had taken off, Cooper had ordered that the rear doorway be left open. The crew had convinced him that it would be impossible for the plane to take off with the exit door open. Cooper allowed it to remain shut. The skyjacked plane had been in the air only 30 minutes when the crew noticed a light on their control panel indicating that the rear door had been opened. When the plane landed in Reno, Nevada, the crew realized that the man was gone.

D. B. Cooper has never been seen again. His crime remains the only unsolved skyjacking.

Cooper had jumped into a storm with strong winds and freezing rain. The air temperature was hovering around seven degrees Fahrenheit. He probably landed in or near the Columbia River near Vancouver, British Columbia. The only things Cooper had left behind in the jet were eight cigarette butts, two parachutes, and maybe a fingerprint. Of the fingerprints found in the

Searching the area along the Columbia River, where $5,800 of the $200,000 ransom money was found, investigators look for more money, more clues and possibly the remains of the mysterious D.B. Cooper.

airplane, 66 remain unidentified. Former FBI agent Ralph Himmelsbach had tried to follow the plane by helicopter before Cooper jumped. Intrigued by the case, Himmelsbach spent eight years trying to solve it. He has concluded that Cooper died after he jumped from the plane.

In 1980 a child found a bundle of money on the banks of the Columbia River. The money, $5,800, was badly eroded and buried only a few inches beneath the dirt. Only the serial numbers and the pictures of Andrew Jackson were visible on the money. The serial numbers matched those photocopied by the FBI in 1971. Officers theorized that the money had been carried downstream by the river, which had high water levels during 1972.

After Cooper's jump, police had thoroughly searched an area designated as his most likely drop point. After Agent Himmelsbach retired in 1980, the pilot who had been flying Cooper's plane told him that he thought he had flown farther east than was previously known.

The case also caught the interest of a retired army infantryman named Jerry Thomas. Thomas was a drill sergeant and survival instructor. He is certain that Cooper would have been badly injured after his jump, if not killed. He does not think Cooper could have navigated his way through the heavily wooded area. Thomas checked the caves that pockmark the Columbia River area in case Cooper had walked or crawled into one of them for shelter. Thomas found nothing.

Himmelsbach thinks that anyone who would commit such a rash act of air piracy would have never parted with any of the money. He thinks that if Cooper had lived, not one dollar, let alone $5,800, would have escaped his grasp.

Himmelsbach believes that Cooper did a good job planning his crime, but that he definitely was not prepared for the harsh weather into which he jumped.

Cooper was wearing loafers, which would have blown off his feet when he jumped. His business suit would have provided no protection against the freezing temperatures.

Investigators also think that Cooper was probably not planning to meet someone on the ground because his flight path was too random.

The decomposed $5,800 worth of $20 bills found along the Columbia River caused speculation that Cooper had not survived his perilous jump.

Speculation still exists that Cooper could have survived the jump if he had enough training. He was described by witnesses as a man almost six feet tall, in his late 40s. Although he drank a lot of whiskey and smoked many cigarettes in the short time on the plane before his jump, he appeared to be physically fit.

Cooper talked in obscenities, leading to speculation that he may have been an ex-con who conceived the idea for his escapade after hearing about a man in Montana who had attempted the same sort of skyjacking. That man had used a gun to threaten the crewmembers and was tackled and captured before he got his hands on any money.

D. B. Cooper has become a folk hero about whom songs have been written and a movie made. An annual D. B. Cooper celebration is held in the town of Ariel, which is near the area where Cooper might have landed. Salt Lake City has a restaurant named after him. There are D. B. Cooper T-shirts and, for whatever reason, bowling competitions have been held in his honor.

Is it so strange that a bandit who kidnapped an airliner should become a hero to many Americans? If D. B. Cooper survived his parachute jump into a storm while wearing only street clothes, he would have absconded with $200,000 of ransom money and thwarted the FBI. In the present era of television news anchors viewed as celebrities, politicians who rely upon public opinion polls instead of conscience, and heroes being made of movie and television actors doing nothing more than reading a script, is it so strange that some people see D. B. Cooper as the real thing? Apparently with no help from anyone, he stole an airliner, perhaps jumped to safety with $200,000 in his pocket, and he harmed no one in the process.

President Theodore Roosevelt once said that, "Only those who dare to fail greatly ever succeed greatly." Perhaps those Americans who have made D. B. Cooper a folk hero do not really admire him for being one of this country's great thieves. Instead, they admire D. B. Cooper for having so dared to fail.

As a result of Cooper's escapade, changes have been made on airline doors and escape hatches, so they can never be opened while aircraft are in flight. And because of this skyjacking, and the 147 others that took place between 1967 and 1972, much improved security measures are in place at most airports around the world, including the use of metal scanners and mandatory luggage checks.

Will the mystery of D. B. Cooper's disappearance ever be solved? Did his body erode with his money? Or is he still living and enjoying the fruits of his FBI loot?

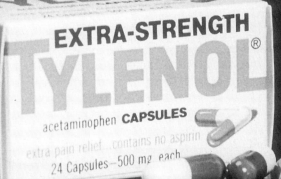

The Tylenol Murders

Mary Kellerman, 12 years old, lived with her parents in Elk Grove Village, Illinois. Early one morning in 1982, she woke her parents and complained of not feeling well. Her parents gave Mary an Extra-Strength Tylenol capsule and put her back to bed. Within hours Mary was dead.

That same morning, Adam Janus sought relief from some minor chest pains. The 27-year-old resident of Arlington Heights, Illinois, took some Extra-Strength Tylenol. An hour later he suffered from cardiopulmonary collapse and died.

Janus's family gathered in sorrow at his home that evening. His brother, Stanley, who was 25, and Stanley's wife, Theresa, went to Adam's medicine cabinet and each took some Tylenol capsules. Within two days, both were dead.

In the nearby suburb of Winfield, Illinois, Mary

Extra-Strength Tylenol capsules were poisoned with cyanide and left on store shelves for unsuspecting victims in the Chicago area in 1982.

Reiner was recovering from the effects of giving birth to her fourth child. She, too, sought the aid of two Tylenol capsules that soon killed her.

Paula Prince, a flight attendant with United Airlines, failed to appear for work. She was found dead in her Chicago apartment. An open bottle of Extra-Strength Tylenol was found near her body.

The seventh Tylenol victim was Mary McFarland, who died in suburban Elmhurst, Illinois.

The cause of these deaths remained a mystery until two off-duty firemen drew the correct conclusion. Two of the police radio dispatches had mentioned that the victims had taken Tylenol. The two firemen went to their superiors with the theory that Tylenol was implicated in the mysterious deaths.

Investigation showed that the Tylenol had been laced with cyanide, and the poisoned capsules had been placed at six different locations: three food stores, two drugstores, and one unidentified location. Apparently, the killer had collected uncontaminated Tylenol packages from various stores. After placing poison in the capsules, he or she distributed the now deadly Tylenol to the six stores. Some of the packages recovered after the murders contained fewer than five poison capsules.

As soon as Tylenol was definitively connected to the seven deaths, a media blitz began. The entire nation was warned about the dangers of using the product. Chicago police drove through the streets, using loudspeakers to warn the public of possible disaster if they took Tylenol. The federal Food and Drug Administration advised the country to avoid the medicine until a complete investigation was undertaken.

Facing a severe and costly public-relations disaster, Johnson & Johnson, the makers of Tylenol, took swift action to ease the public's fears of their product. The company immediately warned consumers to avoid using Tylenol. Production and advertising of the product was immediately stopped and a massive recall was ordered.

More than $100 million worth of Tylenol was pulled from shelves throughout the nation. Johnson & Johnson was praised for being so consumer conscious when risking the loss of such a large amount of profit. An article in the *Washington Post* also praised Johnson & Johnson for being honest with the public. The company never did anything to dissociate its product from the seven deaths. In fact, Johnson & Johnson joined

After seven people in the Chicago area died from the poison capsules, Tylenol was pulled from store shelves nationwide.

James Lewis claimed to have committed the murders but later denied any crime except extortion.

the search to find the answers and posted a $100,000 reward for the capture of the Tylenol murderer.

Johnson & Johnson maintained its good standing with the American public. Robert Wood Johnson, who had held the reins of Johnson & Johnson since the mid-1940s, based his company's actions on its responsibility to "consumers and medical professionals using its products, employees, the communities where its people work and live, and its stockholders."

Investigators found the amount of cyanide in each

capsule to be 65 milligrams. Since death can be caused by as little as 5 to 7 micrograms of cyanide, the victims received amounts that were about 10,000 times the lethal dose. The killer had removed all of the medicine from 20 to 30 capsules and refilled them with the potassium cyanide.

Investigators wondered why the victims had not noticed that the packages of medicine they had bought had been altered. Poisoned packages retrieved from stores after the murders showed obvious signs of tampering. But before the Tylenol murders, America had not been exposed to such a random threat. So the deformed appearance of the tampered packages would probably not have concerned the average consumer.

Investigators deduced that the killer's sloppiness probably revealed the work of an amateur with limited abilities. This idea was also supported by the fact that he grossly overestimated the amount of cyanide necessary to cause death.

Using police "profiling," the science of determining characteristics of an unknown suspect, experts devised a profile on this killer. Investigators assumed he was a white male, in his twenties at the time of the deaths, living in the Chicago area. He was probably a skilled shoplifter, the method most likely used to procure the original packages. Police believed he had average or low intelligence, although he was capable of clever deviousness. They thought he had few friends, like most of those involved with deviant behavior, and that he was employed in a low-skill job. Whatever his motive in carrying out the murders, police believed that he was unsuccessful in achieving that end. He might have hoped to gain infamy from the crimes, but since no claims of responsibility were made by anyone to the press or to the police (as in the Zodiac murders), it seems this goal was not achieved.

Investigations showed that no known person or persons profited monetarily from the deaths of the

Tamper-resistant packaging was mandated after the Tylenol murders, but here David Clare, president of Johnson & Johnson, warns the U.S. Senate that there is no such thing as completely tamper-proof packaging.

seven victims. It is thought the killer might have had a simple hatred of people.

While no one has ever been charged with the Tylenol murders, a man named James Lewis attempted to ride the coattails of the publicity with an extortion scheme. Lewis was a former tax accountant who, in the midst of the scare, sent a letter to Johnson & Johnson demanding $1 million to stop the killings. He was caught and given a 20-year prison sentence. He served 13 years. Lewis denied any responsibility for the deaths and law enforcement found no evidence linking him to the real crimes.

The American public has experienced a long-term effect from these Tylenol murders. Tamper-resistant packaging for all over-the-counter drugs was ordered by the Food and Drug Administration to protect consumers.

Despite these precautions, there have been copycat cases, as often happens with notorious crimes. Product tampering has occurred in various parts of the nation, generally with food or medicinal products. Three times in 1986, this tampering caused deaths. Three consumers who bought Lipton Cup-of-Soup, Exedrin, and once again Tylenol were killed from poison inserted into these products. A contaminated dose of Sudafed decongestant killed a person in 1991 and poisoned Goody's Headache Powder caused the death of a consumer in 1992.

No one has ever been charged with the Chicago Tylenol murders. The killer remains free and unknown.

THE SUNSET LIMITED SABOTAGE

On October 9, 1995, about 60 miles southwest of Phoenix, all was well with the 248 Amtrak passengers and 20-member train crew traveling on the Sunset Limited. But at 1:30 A.M., while crossing a section of desert called Hyder, Arizona, disaster struck.

British Columbia resident Joyce Mathews recalled the moment of terror shared with her young daughter, Brynn: "We were both awakened at the same time by this violent shaking, the car began to twist and turn. It was slowly moving and shaking and suddenly, boom! It just went bang and it stopped. We were very lucky. We've seen a lot of injured people."

"He hit his brakes," another passenger said of the engineer. "In a couple of seconds we were turning over and—bang—we were on the bottom of the creek."

Two engines and eight cars of the train derailed. Four of the cars fell off a 15-foot trestle, crashing into the ravine below.

The Sunset Limited sped toward disaster on the night of October 9, 1995, derailing because of sabotaged tracks.

A rescue worker carries an injured child from the Amtrak train derailment (above) as others try to comfort an injured woman awaiting transport (right). Injured passengers were transported by helicopters to a staging area about six miles away from the crash site.

Mitchell Bates, 41, a sleeping-car attendant employed by Amtrak, was killed. Seventy-eight others were injured. Rescuing the survivors proved a difficult task. The injured had to be taken to a staging area several miles away by medivac helicopters. The Hyder, Arizona, crash site was a remote and desolate area surrounded on three sides by the Gila Bend Mountains. "Every time we put more than three in an ambulance, the wheels sink into the ground," said a rescue worker.

Evidence of sabotage of the train tracks was immediately apparent.

"When the first officer arrived on the scene, the engineer ran up to him—you could hear him shouting over the radio—telling the officer he thought it was sabotage," a fire department dispatcher said. Television

Investigators examine the tampered track. Two notes found at the scene claimed responsibility for the sabotage in the name of a group calling itself "Sons of the Gestapo."

crews that arrived early on the scene recorded a section of broken rail. A coiled red wire lay nearby.

The Sunset Limited had derailed after it hit a section of rail missing a joint bar. The joint bar had been removed just ahead of the 15-foot trestle above the ravine. Twenty-nine spikes had also been pulled from the track. Red wire had been used to connect the tracks, preventing any warning to the engineer about a break.

The FBI was called in and they named the case "Splitrail." In Maricopa County, Arizona, Sheriff Joe

Arpaio said that the crash was believed to be an act of terrorism because of the two notes found on either side of the sabotaged tracks. The notes, addressed to the federal Department of Alcohol, Tobacco and Firearms (ATF), the FBI, the state police, and the sheriff's office, were signed, "Sons of the Gestapo." Although the complete contents of these notes were not revealed by authorities, law enforcement officials said the writers referred to the Waco, Texas, affair.

The Waco incident had occurred in 1993. A religious sect called the Branch Davidians, led by a self-proclaimed leader calling himself David Koresh, had fortified itself in a compound. Koresh claimed he was Jesus Christ. He and his followers went head-to-head with the ATF and other federal authorities over alleged gun violations. Officials also believed that children held within the compound were being sexually abused. In late February ATF agents surrounded the compound to force Koresh to surrender. A fierce shoot-out between law enforcement agents and the Branch Davidian sect broke out on February 28, leaving four ATF agents dead. Then, after a highly publicized, 51-day siege, 80 members of the sect—men, women, and children—were killed in a fiery FBI and ATF assault upon the sect's compound. The fire and deaths of April 19, 1993, ended the siege but began a loud and vocal debate about governmental decision-making.

The notes beside the crumpled train track also referred to the killing of the wife and 14-year-old son of Randy Weaver in August 1992. Weaver and his family had also been under siege by law enforcement officials for Weaver's purported illegal gun activities in Ruby Ridge, Idaho. During the siege Weaver's wife and son were shot. Weaver was eventually taken into custody.

Seven miles from the Sunset Limited crash site the FBI set up a desert command post. The Phoenix FBI office designated Larry McCormick as agent-in-charge of the investigation.

"We are very confident, very sure, we will solve this crime," Agent McCormick said in a desert news conference. The investigation became the biggest crime scene investigation since the April 19, 1995, Oklahoma City bombing of a federal building. Two men were convicted in that case. One was sentenced to death; the other, to life in prison.

FBI agents meticulously combed a square mile surrounding the train crash site. Local law enforcement officials worked with the FBI, looking for footprints, fingerprints on the rails, and tire tracks. Rail pieces were examined to determine the type of tools used to remove the joint bars. Huge cranes removed the derailed train cars from the ravine after they had been thoroughly examined where they lay.

Agents questioned hundreds of local residents, and investigated them to ascertain if any had ties to white supremacist groups. They looked for a man seen near the crash site after the train derailed. An Amtrak employee and two passengers had noticed someone wearing a hat a hundred yards south of the derailment. "At this time," FBI special agent David Tubbs said, "we are treating this person as a witness, not a suspect. I'm here to encourage any possible witness who might have been at the site to come forward and contact us."

The FBI offered a $20,000 reward for information leading to the arrest and conviction of the person or persons responsible for the crash. Initially, the FBI received more than 300 responses to its plea for anyone with information about the crash to come forward. Though some calls came from other parts of the country, most of those wishing to aid the investigation called from the Southwest.

FBI agents also reviewed railroad employment records looking for a disgruntled-employee connection. They found one man who worked for a company that dealt with the railroad and who had allegedly filed a complaint against the railroad. Although a warrant was

The "Sons of the Gestapo" notes cited retaliation for the destruction of the Waco, Texas, compound of David Koresh and his followers (at left) as the reason for the Sunset Limited sabotage.

issued, further investigation showed no evidence linking this man to the Sunset Limited crash.

The two typewritten notes found at the scene were sent to the FBI Laboratory in Washington, D.C., to be tested for fingerprints, residues, and fibers. The notes were then sent to agents specializing in psycholinguistics to determine the type of background and educational level the author might have, or from what part of the country he or she might have come.

The Southern Poverty Law Center in Montgomery,

Right-wing groups like these Nazi skinheads have made Arizona one of their gathering places. But whether one of these groups actually committed the Sunset Limited sabotage is unknown.

Alabama, has a branch called Klanwatch, which tracks hate groups throughout the country. Joe Roy, the director of Klanwatch, said his organization had no record of a group called the Sons of the Gestapo. "This could be Fred-the-farmer who's mad at Amtrak for cutting across his land . . . . It very well could be some disgruntled individual who's trying to blame it on the militias."

After the crash, Senator Jon Kyl of Arizona noted that people had jumped to a premature conclusion about who was to blame when the Oklahoma City bombing occurred. Middle East terrorists were immediately named as the first suspects, which was soon proved incorrect. Kyl said it would be just as premature to blame militia groups for the sabotage of the Sunset Limited.

But Joe Roy said his Klanwatch group was looking into the militia connection because his agency had identified 20 militia groups and 20 white supremacist groups located in Arizona. He said that radical antigovernment and Aryan groups across the nation routinely conduct surveillance of government transportation systems. These groups generate reports that detail precise information about government airlines and rail systems like Amtrak.

Morris Dees, who also works for the Southern Poverty Law Center in Montgomery, Alabama, studies antigovernment hate groups across the country. In 1996, Dees spoke of a plan that had been issued by antigovernment radicals called OPLAN American Viper. "The whole idea behind it is the violent overthrow of the government," Dees said in an Associated Press interview. "It goes into intricate detail how to do that." The 68-page plan outlines how to attack public water supplies, railways, ammunition dumps, airfields, communication lines, and fuel depots.

At the time of the Sunset Limited crash, Arizona was already known as a hotbed for hate groups. Rightwing extremism had long existed in the state, but government officials had noticed a sharp escalation in recruitment by militia groups located throughout the state. Militia leaders credited the upsurge in their memberships to the 1993 siege at Waco. One Arizona militia man, David Espy, considered himself an American revolutionary. He wrote in the Prescott, Arizona, *Courier* that Arizona should secede from the Union. Espy wrote, "I feel a genuine and rational need to form a volunteer militia force, if for no other reason than to let Washington know that there's still a large group of us out here that inherited revolutionary DNA and are willing to fight for it until our dying breath."

David Rosenberg is a member of the Anti-Defamation League of B'nai B'rith located in New York. He keeps track of militia groups for that organization. "Guns are part of the landscape out there," Rosenberg said of Arizona, ". . . it is that atmosphere that makes it easier for those who do want to join these militant, anti-government groups."

In the 1980s, members of a group called the Arizona Patriots had planned to blow up the state's main Internal Revenue Service office, the Palo Verde nuclear power plant, and an abortion clinic in Tucson. They were jailed after an informant revealed the plots to authorities. Media scrutiny of Arizona militia groups increased after it was learned that Timothy McVeigh, convicted of the Oklahoma City bombing, had ties to Kingman, Arizona.

However, the only connection between the dark world of domestic terrorism and the Sunset Limited attack is the notes signed "Sons of the Gestapo," which were found at the scene. But the existence of the notes does not prove the existence of the Sons of the Gestapo. If other acts of sabotage or terrorism have been committed by this group, law enforcement personnel have not told the public. Since portions of these notes have never been released, it is not even possible to link this group with Arizona's well-known popularity among right-wing militia groups. The references to the Waco shoot-out found in the notes may be the only presumed mark of right-wing survivalist groups. Until more of the note contents are released to the public, until the Sons of the Gestapo again get the blood of innocent citizens on their hands, or until someone is convicted of the Sunset Limited attack, law enforcement and civic organizations will continue to carefully watch and monitor Arizona's radical groups that promote hatred and violence.

After years of investigation, the FBI has still made no arrests in the sabotage of the Amtrak Sunset Limited. The mystery of who pulled the spikes from the track remains an unsolved case, generating more questions than answers.

THE ASSASSINATION OF PRESIDENT KENNEDY

Every American born during the first quarter of the 20th century remembers precisely where he or she was when the Sunday afternoon radio programming was interrupted by a news flash that Japanese airplanes had bombed Pearl Harbor at daybreak Hawaii time, December 7, 1941.

Every American born during the first half of the 20th century remembers precisely where he or she was when the Friday afternoon soap operas on television were interrupted by the news flash that shots had been fired at the Dallas, Texas, motorcade of President John F. Kennedy, on November 22, 1963. In the space of five seconds—about seven heartbeats—the president of the United States was dead.

Dressed in a pink suit, Mrs. Kennedy was waving to the crowd on her left at 12:30 P.M., Dallas time. The

The motorcade of President John F. Kennedy, moments before shots rang out in Dallas, Texas, November 22, 1963.

president waved at her side in the back seat of the presidential car as it traveled 11 miles per hour through sunlit Dealey Plaza. Texas governor John Connally and his wife, Nellie, rode in the front seat of the car. The motorcade turned down Elm Street toward a highway underpass. Ahead and to the right was a green hill known as the Grassy Knoll. Behind the hill stood a wooden fence with a parking lot and railroad yard behind it. Slightly behind the president's car, and to the right, stood the Texas School Book Depository building. A few windows in its six stories were open.

Suddenly Mrs. Kennedy heard a loud crack echo through Dealey Plaza. She turned to look at her husband. The president clutched at his throat and he had a questioning expression on his face. Two or three more gunshots erupted and John F. Kennedy's head exploded, showering his wife's pink suit with bone fragments and bloody brain tissue. One bullet plowed into Governor Connally's back and punched through his chest, shattering his right arm and digging into his thigh.

Secret Service agent William Greer stood on the gas pedal of the presidential limousine and sped toward Parkland Memorial Hospital, only five minutes away. Secret Service agent Clinton Hill had been standing on the running board of the car directly behind the Kennedy-Connally car. When the shots rang out and Agent Hill saw the president grab his neck, Hill dove toward the president's car. Hill climbed the rear bumper. John Kennedy's bloodstained wife stood in the back seat and reached across the trunk to pick up a piece of her husband's skull. She helped Agent Hill climb into the back seat where he covered the dying president with his own body.

Clinton Hill's bold heroics were just five seconds too late. When they reached the hospital, President John Kennedy was pronounced dead from a massive gunshot wound to the head.

Barely an hour earlier, Julia Ann Mercer had been

driving her car along the street that the president of the United States was about to travel. Turning onto Elm Street, she had been forced to stop because a pickup truck was illegally parked by the Grassy Knoll. As she waited for traffic to start moving, she saw two men in the truck. The passenger in the green pickup got out, carrying what Julia Mercer thought was a gun case. The man then walked up the Grassy Knoll.

As the motorcade approached, Lee Bowers was near the railroad yard behind the Grassy Knoll, where he worked for the Union Terminal Company directing railroad traffic in the switching yard. Bowers had stopped working long enough to watch President Kennedy and Governor Connally drive past. When

Jacqueline Kennedy turns to her gravely injured husband as the sound of gunfire echoes through Dealey Plaza in Dallas.

Seconds after the shooting, the cameraman at left and the four spectators ducking for cover have turned toward the Grassy Knoll— the direction from which shots came, according to many eyewitnesses.

Bowers heard the sound of gunfire or firecrackers, he glanced to the area behind the fence on the Grassy Knoll. He saw a flash or a puff of smoke near the fence.

When Lee Bowers looked at the fence at the moment of the assassination, J. C. Price was doing the same thing. He saw a man running from the knoll, back toward the railroad yard. The running man carried something in his hand.

S. M. Holland was standing on the highway overpass, looking up Elm Street to watch the motorcade approach. Like Lee Bowers, Holland worked for the railroad. When he heard the sound of gunshots, he looked to his left toward the Grassy Knoll. He saw a puff of smoke near the fence.

Secret Service agent Paul E. Landis Jr. was guarding the car just behind the presidential limousine when the first shot sounded. He thought that the shot came from in front of the president's car.

By the time Dallas police officer J. M. Smith arrived at the Grassy Knoll moments after the shooting, he could smell the pungent scent of gunpowder in the air behind the fence.

When the motorcade climbed the slight incline of Elm Street in front of the Texas School Book Depository building, Harold L. Brennan was sitting across Elm Street and was waiting to see the president. Brennan saw a man at an open window on the sixth floor of the Book Depository. When Brennan heard the first gunshot, he looked up at the open window and saw a man fire a rifle, then disappear.

Less than an hour after the shooting, a Dallas police officer was shot dead in his patrol car a few blocks from the assassination scene. Within another hour, Dallas police arrested a 24-year-old man for the policeman's murder. The suspect was Lee Harvey Oswald, who had worked in the Book Depository building for only five weeks before that bloody Friday afternoon. Oswald denied killing the police officer and, when asked, he denied knowing anything about the killing of the president and the wounding of Governor Connally. By 7:00 P.M. Friday night, Oswald was charged with the murder of officer J. D. Tippit. And by 1:30 Saturday morning, he was charged with the murder of President Kennedy. Three days later, Oswald was shot and killed in the basement of the Dallas police station in front of a live television audience of millions. He was gunned down by Jack Ruby, a nightclub owner connected to the Dallas underworld.

One week after Kennedy's death, President Lyndon

Lee Harvey Oswald was taken into custody by the Dallas police and charged with the assassination. He would not live to stand trial or tell his story.

B. Johnson issued an executive order creating a blue-ribbon commission to investigate the Kennedy murder. Chaired by the chief justice of the United States, Earl Warren, the investigation would be known forever as the Warren Commission.

The Warren Commission set to work to decide if Lee Harvey Oswald, now dead, did assassinate the president and wound Governor Connally. The commission also had to decide if Oswald acted alone or was part of a conspiracy. Ten months later, the commission issued its formal report. The members did so, they said, "in recognition of the right of people everywhere to full and truthful knowledge concerning these events."

The Warren Commission submitted its report, which would prove to be quite controversial, to President Johnson on September 24, 1964.

Few of the "facts" that the Warren Commission presented as settled have actually remained settled. Scholarly books, tabloid books, television documentaries, and screen reenactments of the assassination have become a cottage industry. Most of these reports and documentaries challenge the findings of the Warren Commission. Some challenges are grounded in real forensic science and objective investigation; many are grounded in fantasy, inspired by a quick dollar.

The Warren Commission records, files, witness interviews, and official documents fill 363 cubic feet of space in the National Archives and Records Administration complex in College Park, Maryland. According to the Warren Commission, Lee Harvey Oswald acted alone. He used a 23-year-old Italian rifle to fire at least three shots at the presidential car. One shot missed; one shot hit President Kennedy in the upper back, near his neck, exited through the president's throat, and then struck Governor Connally in the back. The third shot struck the back of the president's head, blowing out the right side of his skull and nearly half of his brain. All the shots were fired from the sixth-floor, southeast window of the Texas School Book Depository building—the window where Howard Brennan had seen the rifle on November 22.

Were the Warren Commission's 1964 report the last word on the presidential assassination, the death of John F. Kennedy would not be an unsolved crime. But the commission was only the first word of a controversy that has raged for almost 40 years and that will continue well into the 21st century.

In its most controversial conclusion, the Warren Commission ruled that, "Although it is not necessary to any essential findings of the Commission to determine just which shot hit Governor Connally, there is very persuasive evidence from the experts to indicate that the same bullet which pierced the president's throat also caused Governor Connally's wounds."

Members of the Warren Commission begin their inquiry, December 5, 1963.

From the moment the Warren Commission issued its report, not even President Lyndon Johnson believed it. President Johnson was so certain that Oswald was part of a broader conspiracy that he privately ordered a second, top-secret investigation by Richard Helms, then deputy director of the Central Intelligence Agency. The secret investigation was completed and presented to President Johnson. That CIA report is still a classified secret and it has never been released to the public.

Controversy also swirls around the official autopsy performed upon President Kennedy's body through the night of November 22. The autopsy was performed by officers of the United States Navy at the National

Naval Medical Center, Bethesda, Maryland. Commander Dr. James J. Humes, chief pathologist at the naval hospital, examined the president's body. Humes had little experience doing autopsies. He found that three-quarters of the right side of President Kennedy's brain had been destroyed. Commander Humes found the bullet hole in the president's back, but a navy officer ordered Dr. Humes not to dissect the wound to trace the path of the bullet.

The navy pathologist was puzzled that there was no evidence of where the bullet had lodged after hitting President Kennedy in the back. X rays showed no bullet inside the president's body. Commander Humes probed the back wound with his finger and found nothing. He assumed that a shallow bullet had probably been pushed out of its hole when emergency room doctors had been working furiously to save the president's life at Parkland Hospital in Dallas.

But even this lack of a bullet at the autopsy is puzzling to commission critics. In the assassination records at the National Archives, there is a written receipt from the FBI for a "missile recovered by Commander James Humes." There is also a written record that the Secret Service received the FBI's receipt for the bullet removed from the president's body. If a bullet had been found at the autopsy, then no bullet could have passed through President Kennedy to hit the governor—which means a second assassin was at work that day.

The commission concluded, "The autopsy disclosed the large head wound observed at Parkland and the wound in the front of the neck which had been enlarged by the Parkland doctors when they performed the tracheotomy."

The commission report reads as if there were only one report by Dr. Humes for his presidential autopsy. But there were two reports. Commander Humes burned the first report in the fireplace in his own home in the early morning hours of November 23.

Dr. Humes wrote his first autopsy report on the government form stained with the blood of the dead president. Early Saturday morning, he telephoned Dr. Malcolm Perry, the Parkland surgeon who had attended the president in Dallas. Only then did Commander Humes learn that Dr. Perry had sliced an incision in the president's throat for a breathing tube at the exact location of an apparent bullet hole. Commander Humes destroyed his first report and rewrote it to show an exit wound in the president's throat for the bullet that had entered the president's back.

No one can explain why the "official" photographs of the president's head wound and the X rays of his skull at the autopsy do not quite match. X rays of the head show that the president's forehead and right eye socket were destroyed by the gunfire. But official autopsy photographs show no such massive destruction of the president's face. History professor Michael L. Kurtz, of Southeast Louisiana University at Hammond, has written that these photographs and X rays "simply cannot be of the same individual taken at the same time."

Much criticism of the Warren Commission report concerns the medical evidence. Not only was the original autopsy report destroyed by Commander Humes, but also much evidence is missing from the National Archives. The president's brain, removed at the autopsy, is lost; tissue slides made of the edges of the president's back wound have been lost; an entire roll of film shot during the autopsy was deliberately destroyed; all photographs of the president's brain after its removal from his body are missing; and all X rays of the president's arms and legs are missing. While this does not necessarily mean there was a massive conspiracy to tamper with evidence, it does mean that future generations of historians and medical experts can never analyze the original medical documentation and evidence.

But the single greatest controversy created by the Warren Commission report is the single-bullet theory,

Lee Harvey Oswald was said to have stood in the window indicated by the arrow and fired three rounds into President John F. Kennedy's motorcade.

X ray of the front of President Kennedy's skull taken during his autopsy. The X ray shows the president's forehead destroyed, but official autopsy photos show no such destruction.

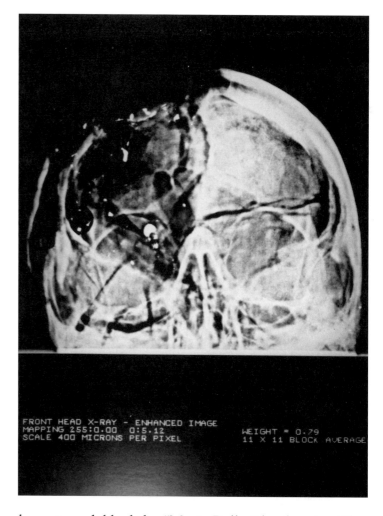

FRONT HEAD X-RAY - ENHANCED IMAGE
MAPPING 255:0.00 0:5.12   WEIGHT = 0.79
SCALE 400 MICRONS PER PIXEL   11 X 11 BLOCK AVERAGE

long-since dubbed the "Magic Bullet" by skeptics. The commission was faced with a grave problem of evidence and timing. If Lee Harvey Oswald acted alone in his murderous deed, then he had to have fired all of the rifle bullets that struck President Kennedy and Governor Connally.

Waiting to see the president drive down Elm Street that sunny day in Dallas was Abraham Zapruder. When the presidential car drove slowly past him, Mr. Zapruder took home movies with his 8 mm camera. Through its eyepiece, he saw and recorded the president's head explode. Forensic experts who examined each frame of the Zapruder film determined an exact timeline for the shooting. Each movie frame is a snapshot of 1/18th of a second. Counting the frames between the first reactions of the victims as they were shot gave the Warren Commission a precise sequence of the rifle fire. Therein was the problem discovered by a commission aide, attorney Arlen Specter from Pennsylvania, who was later elected to the United States Senate.

The famous Zapruder film showed only seven-tenths of a second between the president's first reaction to being struck in the back and Governor Connally's reaction to a bullet through his back. FBI marksmen needed at least 2.25 seconds to cycle the old-fashioned bolt on Oswald's rifle, to load a new cartridge, and then to aim and fire. So there was a serious timing problem for the commission. If the president and the governor were struck by two different but almost simultaneous bullets, then someone else had to be shooting with Oswald. Attorney Specter came up with the solution: only one bullet hit both men—it went through the president's neck into the governor's back.

Commission critics quickly attacked the single-bullet theory. So did Governor Connally and Mrs. Connally. Both agreed that they heard two separate shots a heartbeat apart: one hit the president and the second struck the governor. All of the surgeons who worked to save Governor Connally's life at Parkland Hospital, including Dr. Robert Shaw and Dr. Thomas Shires, agreed that the governor had to have been hit by a bullet that had not struck anything before wounding him.

Even the Secret Service initially believed as early as November 28 that two separate bullets hit the two men. The FBI believed that the governor was hit by a separate bullet, and the whole commission agreed up to April 22, 1964, when the single-bullet theory was created. Critics of the Warren Commission argue that President Johnson wanted the commission to conclude that

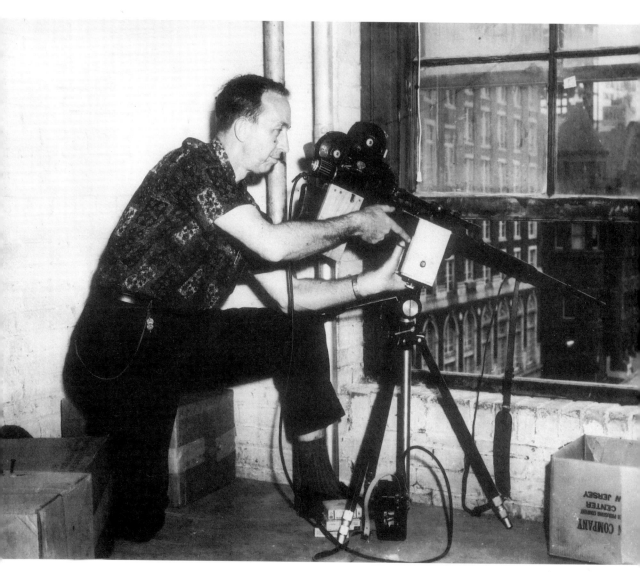

An FBI agent reenacts the shooting from the Texas School Book Depository, trying to determine if Lee Harvey Oswald had time to fire all the shots.

Oswald was not part of a conspiracy. This would protect the American people from national outrage or panic, and more important, it would prevent a national cry for retaliation if indeed there had been a conspiracy by foreign governments. Commission critics insist that the Warren Commission found that Lee Harvey Oswald killed the president and that he acted alone only because that is the conclusion the commission wanted to reach.

By adopting the single-bullet theory, the Warren Commission had to summarily discard the eyewitness accounts of a gunman on the Grassy Knoll or in more than one window of the Book Depository. Of 75 witnesses in Dealey Plaza who were later interviewed, at least 39 heard or saw a shot fired from the Grassy Knoll.

The Warren Commission candidly admitted that it concluded Oswald did all of the shooting that Friday afternoon since "the three used cartridge cases found near the window on the sixth floor at the southeast corner of the [Texas School Book Depository] building were fired from the same rifle which fired the above-described bullet and fragments, to the exclusion of all other weapons."

The "above-described bullet" is the now infamous Warren Commission Exhibit 399. It is a bullet of the kind fired by the type of rifle found on the sixth floor at the Book Depository: a 1940-vintage Mannlicher-Carcano rifle chambered for 6.5 mm bullets.

The Warren Commission had before it a nearly perfect 6.5 mm rifle bullet, which the commission concluded was "found on Governor Connally's stretcher at Parkland Memorial Hospital." But later research by commission critics has confirmed that this bullet was found on a stretcher in a hospital hallway, not on the stretcher used to transport either President Kennedy or Governor Connally. That much is fairly certain now. Forensic tests on Exhibit 399 did confirm that the bullet had been fired from the Italian rifle found in the Book Depository. But no one knows when that bullet was fired or where. Oswald was seen target shooting at a Dallas rifle range. The bullet might have been taken from that site and "planted" in the hospital corridor. This is a favorite theme of conspiracy buffs. When Warren Commission experts fired Oswald's rifle with 6.5 mm ammunition into goats and human cadavers, the bullets were badly deformed by the impact. But Exhibit 399 was nearly perfect, even though the single-bullet advocates assert that it passed through President Kennedy's neck, went through Governor Connally's back and wrist, and lodged in his leg. Exhibit 399 is credited with inflicting seven wounds, without deforming.

There is also fodder for skeptics in the commission's reference to the three spent cartridge cases located by the sixth-floor window where the assassin supposedly fired. Later tests of the scratches, marks, and deformation of each empty cartridge case confirm that only one of the three rounds, Commission Exhibit 544, was actually fired from the rifle allegedly owned by Oswald. The other two cases had been in the rifle but they had never been fired from the rifle.

Commission critics point out that none of the three empty cartridges had any fingerprints on them belonging to Oswald. In the alleged murder rifle, the cartridges are loaded into the rifle on a clip, as compared to a sealed magazine. There were no Oswald fingerprints on the clip either. Critics question who loaded the rifle used to shoot the president.

The Warren Commission clearly traced the rifle found in the Book Depository to a mail-order rifle purchased by Lee Harvey Oswald. The commission regarded that rifle's serial number, C-2766, as unique in all the world. But it is not. Ten different companies made Mannlicher-Carcano rifles for Italy during World War II—and all 10 manufacturers made a serial number C-2766.

Almost microscopic analysis of the Zapruder film 20 years after the assassination suggests that at the moment of the shooting, President Kennedy's head made two sharp movements within half a second—one forward, and one violently backward and to the left, between frames 313 and 321 of the film. This suggests to commission critics that the president was shot in the head twice, almost simultaneously: once from behind from the Book Depository, and once from the right side

C.E. 399   8/23/78

from the Grassy Knoll. The Grassy Knoll gunman, it is argued, used an expanding (soft, hollow-point bullet) or exploding bullet, which exploded the president's head at the instant the second shot hit from behind. This shot from the right front would explain why pieces of the president's head were found 20 feet behind and to the left of the presidential car.

So many questions were raised by the Warren Commission that the United States House of Representatives reopened the Kennedy Assassination investigation 15 years later. The House Select Committee on Assassinations reopened the Kennedy and Martin Luther King Jr. assassination investigations. Between 1977 and 1979, the Select Committee amassed 325 cubic feet of documents and records, which now reside at the National Archives at College Park.

The controversial "single bullet," Exhibit 399 for the Warren Commission.

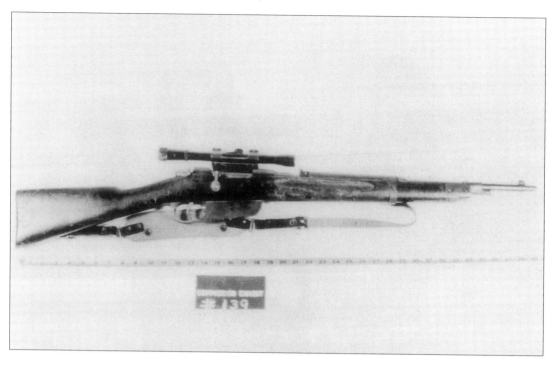

The rifle supposedly used by Lee Harvey Oswald to shoot three bullets at President Kennedy. According to the Warren Commission, one bullet missed, one wounded Kennedy and Governor Connally, and the third hit the president in the head, killing him.

Although the Select Committee accepted most of the Warren Commission's findings, it did conclude that there was indeed a second assassin behind the fence on the Grassy Knoll in Dallas.

But the Select Committee was quickly attacked by critics, since it had also adopted the single-bullet theory. The Select Committee concluded that Lee Harvey Oswald fired three shots, two of which probably hit his target—100 yards away—while the assassin on the Grassy Knoll missed the president from only 16 yards.

Whether one supports the Warren Commission or attacks it, few students of the assassination would claim to know why Lee Harvey Oswald killed President Kennedy—if indeed he killed him. Oswald's daughter had been born October 20, 1963. Why would a new father become a presidential assassin?

The most scholarly overview of the Kennedy assassination was written in 1983 and updated in 1993 by Professor Michael Kurtz. Professor Kurtz argues that "at least three different assassins fired shots at the presidential motorcade." Dr. Kurtz is also doubtful that Oswald fired any of those shots, although he finds the evidence strong that Oswald did kill Officer Tippit.

Professor Kurtz also shares President Lyndon Johnson's belief that President Kennedy's murder was planned and carried out by Cuba's Fidel Castro. President Johnson told television correspondent Howard K. Smith and Cabinet Secretary Joseph Califano that "Kennedy was trying to get Castro; but Castro got him first."

Professor Kurtz notes 20 years worth of CIA and White House efforts to murder Fidel Castro. Among the National Archives collections is the investigation of the Rockefeller Commission in 1975. Created by President Gerald Ford, the Commission to Investigate Central Intelligence Agency Activities created 2,500 pages of documents on the Kennedy assassination, including records of the Kennedy administration's undercover and unlawful attempts to assassinate Fidel Castro.

Kurtz concluded his exhaustive review of the Kennedy assassination this way: "I believe that Fidel Castro ordered the assassination of President Kennedy in retaliation for the repeated assassination attempts against his own life during the Kennedy Administration."

Kurtz, who has devoted 20 years of historical research to the Kennedy assassination, believes that recent forensic analysis of autopsy photographs destroys the single-bullet theory. According to Kurtz, the forensic photo analysis of Kennedy's back wound reveals that the bullet struck the president with a slightly upward angle, while the bullet that entered Governor Connally hit at a downward angle. Because Elm Street is a gentle hill that rises away from the Book Depository, there must have been a rifleman in a window lower than the sixth floor, probably on the second floor, Kurtz believes.

President John F. Kennedy was laid to rest on November 25, 1963, but the controversy and questions surrounding his death may never be resolved.

Using the Zapruder film as his timeline, Professor Kurtz argues that four shots were fired at the presidential limousine by at least three assassins.

The mystery of who killed President Kennedy—the enduring question of late-20th-century America—may linger well into the next century. Those who believe the Warren Commission already know that Lee Harvey Oswald did it, acting alone. Those who do not believe the Warren Commission insist that the killer or killers of the 35th president of the United States are still at large. That the Internet has more than 200 sites devoted to the Kennedy assassination proves that public interest has not waned in 40 years.

Among those scholars who do not believe in the ultimate conclusions of the Warren Commission is Professor Kurtz. He wrote, "It is an unsolved mystery. . . . [T]hose responsible for the murder of John Kennedy got away with it."

Maybe.

Further Reading

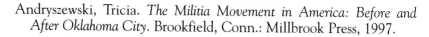

Andryszewski, Tricia. *The Militia Movement in America: Before and After Oklahoma City.* Brookfield, Conn.: Millbrook Press, 1997.

Begg, Paul; Martin Fido; and Keith Skinner. *The Jack the Ripper A-Z.* London: Headline Book Publishing, 1996.

Douglas, John, and Mark Olshaker. *Mind Hunter.* New York: Pocket Books, 1995.

Fletcher, Connie. *What Cops Know.* New York: Pocket Books, 1994.

Graysmith, Robert. *Zodiac.* New York: Berkley Books, 1987.

Gunther, Max. *D. B. Cooper: What Really Happened?* Chicago: Contemporary Books, 1986.

"John F. Kennedy Assassination Records Collection." National Archives and Records Administration. Available from http://www.nara.gov/nara/jfk/gil_42.html.

Kurtz, Michael L. *Crime of the Century: The Kennedy Assassination from a Historian's Perspective.* 2d ed. Knoxville: University of Tennessee Press, 1983, 1993.

McGuckin, Frank, ed. *Terrorism in the United States.* New York: H. W. Wilson, 1997.

Rhodes, Bernie, and Russell P. Calame. *D. B. Cooper, the Real McCoy.* Salt Lake City: University of Utah Press, 1991.

Samenow, Stanton E. *Inside the Criminal Mind.* New York: Times Books, 1984.

"The Warren Report, Chapter 1." Available from http://www.informatik.uni-rostock.de/ Kennedy/WCR/wcr1.html.

Wilson, Kirk. *Unsolved Great True Crimes of the 20th Century.* New York: Carroll and Graf, 1991.

Index

Tumblety, Francis, 27-29
Tylenol, Extra-Strength, 14
    poisoning of, 50, 52-53
    recall of, 50-51
Tylenol killer,
    copycat crimes, 55
    cyanide and, 52-53
    modus operandi, 14-15
    profile of, 53-54
    reward for capture of, 52
    seven victims of, 49-50

U.S. Naval Intelligence, 33

Vallejo Times–Herald, 33

Waco, Texas, affair, 61, 66
Warren Commission, 16,
    17, 74-76, 77, 78, 80,
    81, 82-83, 84, 86, 88
Warren Commission
    Exhibit 399, 83-84, 85
Warren Commission
    Exhibit 544, 84
Warren, Earl, 74
Watkins, P. C., 22
Weaver, Randy, 61
Whitechapel Vigilance
    Committee, 24

Zapruder, Abraham, 80
Zapruder film, 80-81, 84,
    87-88
Zodiac killer, 14, 15, 30
    communication from,
        33-35, 36-37
    modus operandi, 15
    profile of, 36
    suspects in the killings
        by, 38-39
    threats from, 36-37
    victims of, 14, 31-32, 35

PHELAN POWELL wrote for a college newspaper in Boston for which she also created a cartoon strip. As a journalism student, she wrote feature articles for the University of Maryland *Diamondback*. As a Coast Guard Reservist, she worked in the Public Affairs office and dealt with press relations. Powell has also worked as a correspondent for the daily *Michigan City News-Dispatch*. She has written three other titles for Chelsea House Publishers.

AUSTIN SARAT is William Nelson Cromwell Professor of Jurisprudence and Political Science at Amherst College, where he also chairs the Department of Law, Jurisprudence and Social Thought. Professor Sarat is the author or editor of 23 books and numerous scholarly articles. Among his books are *Law's Violence*, *Sitting in Judgment: Sentencing the White Collar Criminal*, and *Justice and Injustice in Law and Legal Theory*. He has received many academic awards and held several prestigious fellowships. He is President of the Law & Society Association and Chair of the Working Group on Law, Culture and Humanities. In addition, he is a nationally recognized teacher and educator whose teaching has been featured in the *New York Times*, on the *Today* show, and on National Public Radio's *Fresh Air*.

Picture Credits